The Complete Poems

By Anne Sexton

Anne Sexton

The Complete Poems

_____

With a foreword by
Maxine Kumin

A Mariner Book

HOUGHTON MIFFLIN COMPANY
BOSTON • NEW YORK

First Mariner Books edition 1999

Library of Congress Cataloging-in-Publication Data
Sexton, Anne.
The complete poems.
Includes index.
I. Title.
PS3537.E915A17   1981   811'.54   81-2482
ISBN 0-395-29475-4   AACR2
ISBN 0-395-95776-1 (pbk.)

Printed in the United States of America

QUM 10 9 8 7 6 5 4 3 2 1

A Note on the Text

THIS VOLUME contains all the poems in the eight books that Anne Sexton sent to press in her lifetime, as well as the poems from the two collections prepared for publication after her death. A few poems written in the last year of her life are collected here for the first time.

For reasons of space, the stories originally included in *The Book of Folly* and in *Words for Dr. Y.* have not been republished here; nor has it been possible to include Kurt Vonnegut's preface or Barbara Swan's drawings for *Transformations*.

I would like to thank the many friends of Anne Sexton's poetry who have contributed in so many ways over the years to both the creation and publication of her work.

Linda Gray Sexton

Contents

ALL MY PRETTY ONES (1962)

    I

LIVE OR DIE (1966)

LOVE POEMS (1969)

THE AWFUL ROWING TOWARD GOD (1975)

POSTHUMOUSLY PUBLISHED WORK

45 MERCY STREET (1976)

I. BEGINNING THE HEGIRA

II. BESTIARY U.S.A.

LAST POEMS

How It Was

Maxine Kumin on Anne Sexton

ANNE SEXTON as I remember her on our first meeting in the late
winter of 1957, tall, blue-eyed, stunningly slim, her carefully coifed
dark hair decorated with flowers, her face skillfully made up, looked
every inch the fashion model. And indeed she had briefly modeled
for the Hart Agency in Boston. Earrings and bracelets, French
perfume, high heels, matching lip and fingernail gloss bedecked
her, all intimidating sophistications in the chalk-and-wet-overshoes
atmosphere of the Boston Center for Adult Education, where we
were enrolled in John Holmes's poetry workshop. Poetry — we
were both ambitious beginners — and proximity — we lived in
the same suburb — brought us together. As intimate friends and
professional allies, we remained intensely committed to one
another's writing and well-being to the day of her death in the
fall of 1974.

The facts of Anne Sexton's troubled and chaotic life are well
known; no other American poet in our time has cried aloud pub-
licly so many private details. While the frankness of these revela-
tions attracted many readers, especially women, who identified
strongly with the female aspect of the poems, a number of poets
and critics — for the most part, although not exclusively, male
— took offense. For Louis Simpson, writing in *Harper's Magazine*,

"Menstruation at Forty" was "the straw that broke this camel's back." And years before he wrote his best-selling novel, *Deliverance*, which centers on a graphic scene of homosexual rape, James Dickey, writing in the *New York Times Book Review*, excoriated the poems in *All My Pretty Ones*, saying "It would be hard to find a writer who dwells more insistently on the pathetic and disgusting aspects of bodily experience..." In a terse eulogy Robert Lowell declared, with considerable ambivalence it would seem, "For a book or two, she grew more powerful. Then writing was too easy or too hard for her. She became meager and exaggerated. Many of her most embarrassing poems would have been fascinating if someone had put them in quotes, as the presentation of some character, not the author." Sexton's work rapidly became a point of contention over which opposing factions dueled in print, at literary gatherings, and in the fastnesses of the college classroom.

And yet the ground for Sexton's confessional poems had been well prepared. In 1956, Allen Ginsberg's *Howl* had declaimed:

I saw the best minds of my generation destroyed by madness,
    starving hysterical naked
· ·
                       ... on the granite steps of
the madhouse with shaven heads and harlequin speech of
suicide, demanding instantaneous lobotomy,
and who were given instead the concrete void of insulin metrasol
electricity hydrotherapy psychotherapy occupational therapy
pingpong & amnesia ...

At the time Sexton began to work in the confessional mode, W. D. Snodgrass had already published his prize-winning collection, *Heart's Needle*, which included details of his divorce and custody struggle. Sylvia Plath and Robert Lowell were hammering out their own autobiographical accounts of alienation, despair, anomie, and madness. John Berryman, deceiving no one, charmingly protested in a prefatory note that the Henry of *The Dream Songs* "is essentially about an imaginary character (not the poet, not me) ... who has suffered an irreversible loss and talks about himself sometimes in the first person, sometimes in the third, sometimes even in the second ...." The use of *le moi* was being cultivated in fashionable literary journals everywhere. It seems curious that the major and by far most vitriolic expressions of outrage were reserved for Sexton.

Someone once said that we have art in order not to die of the truth, a dictum we might neatly apply to Sexton's perspectives. To Hayden Carruth, the poems "raise the never-solved problem of what literature really is, where you draw the line between art and documentary."

While Louise Bogan and Joyce Carol Oates for the most part appraise Sexton favorably, Mona Van Duyn finds Sexton's "delineation of femaleness so fanatical that it makes one wonder, even after many years of being one, what a woman is ...." Muriel Rukeyser, who sees the issue as "survival, piece by piece of the body, step by step of poetic experience, and even more the life entire ...," finds much to praise, for instance singling out "In Celebration of My Uterus" as "one of the few poems in which a woman has come to the fact as symbol, the center after many years of silence and taboo."

Over and over in the critical literature dealing with the body of Sexton's work, we find these diametrical oppositions. The intimate details divulged in Sexton's poetry enchanted or repelled with equal passion. In addition to the strong feelings Anne's work aroused, there was the undeniable fact of her physical beauty. Her presence on the platform dazzled with its staginess, its props of water glass, cigarettes, and ashtray. She used pregnant pauses, husky whispers, pseudoshouts to calculated effect. A Sexton audience might hiss its displeasure or deliver a standing ovation. It did not doze off during a reading.

Anne basked in the attention she attracted, partly because it was antithetical to an earlier generation's view of the woman writer as "poetess," and partly because she was flattered by and enjoyed the adoration of her public. But behind the glamorously garbed woman lurked a terrified and homely child, cowed from the cradle onward, it seemed, by the indifference and cruelties of her world. Her parents, she was convinced, had not wanted her to be born. Her sisters, she alleged, competed against and won out over her. Her teachers, unable to rouse the slumbering intelligence from its hiding place, treated her with impatience and anger. Anne's counterphobic response to rejection and admonishment was always to defy, dare, press, contravene. Thus the frightened little girl became a flamboyant and provocative woman; the timid child who skulked in closets burst forth as an exhibitionist declaiming with her own rock group; the intensely private individual bared her liver to the eagle in public readings where almost invariably there was standing room only.

Born Anne Gray Harvey in 1928, she attended public school in Wellesley, Massachusetts, spent two years at Rogers Hall preparatory school, and then one year at Garland Junior College in Boston. A few months shy of her twentieth birthday, she eloped with Alfred Muller Sexton II (nicknamed Kayo), enrolled in a Hart Agency modeling course, and lived briefly in Baltimore and San Francisco while her husband served in the Navy. In 1953, she returned to Massachusetts, where Linda Gray Sexton was born.

The first breakdown, diagnosed as postpartum depression, occurred in 1954, the same year her beloved great-aunt Anna Ladd Dingley, the Nana of the poems, died. She took refuge in Westwood Lodge, a private neuropsychiatric hospital that was frequently to serve as her sanctuary when the voices that urged her to die reached an insistent pitch. Its director, Dr. Martha Brunner-Orne, figured in Anne's life as a benevolent but disciplinary mother, who would not permit this troubled daughter to kill herself.

Nevertheless, seven months after her second child, Joyce Ladd Sexton, was born in 1955, Anne suffered a second crisis and was hospitalized. The children were sent to live with her husband's parents; and while they were separated from her, she attempted suicide on her birthday, November 9, 1956. This was the first of several episodes, or at least the first that was openly acknowledged. Frequently, these attempts occurred around Anne's birthday, a time of year she came increasingly to dread. Dr. Martin Orne,

Brunner-Orne's son, was the young psychiatrist at Glenside Hospital who attended Anne during this siege and treated her for the next seven years. After administering a series of diagnostic tests, he presented his patient with her scores, objective evidence that, despite the disapproving naysayers from her past, she was highly intelligent. Her associative gifts suggested that she ought to return to the writing of poetry, something she had shown a deft talent for during secondary school. It was at Orne's insistence that Anne enrolled in the Holmes workshop.

"You, Dr. Martin" came directly out of that experience, as did so many of the poems in her first collection, *To Bedlam and Part Way Back*. On a snowy Sunday afternoon early in 1957, she drove to my house to ask me to look at "something." Did she dare present it in class? Could it be called a poem? It was "Music Swims Back to Me," her first breakaway from adolescent lyrics in rhyming iambic pentameter.

Years later, when it seemed to her that all else in her life had failed — marriage, the succor of children, the grace of friendship, the promised land to which psychotherapy held the key — she turned to God, with a kind of stubborn absolutism that was missing from the Protestantism of her inheritance. The God she wanted was a sure thing, an Old Testament avenger admonishing his Chosen People, an authoritarian yet forgiving Father decked out in sacrament and ceremony. An elderly, sympathetic priest she called on — "accosted" might be a better word — patiently explained that he could not make her a Catholic by fiat, nor could he administer the sacrament (the last rites) she longed for. But in his native wisdom he said a saving thing to her, said the magic and simple words that kept her alive at least a year beyond her time and made *The Awful Rowing Toward God* a possibility. "God is in your typewriter," he told her.

I cite these two examples to indicate the influence that figures of authority had over Anne's life in the most elemental sense; first the psychiatrist and then the priest put an imprimatur on poetry as salvation, as a worthy goal in itself. I am convinced that poetry kept Anne alive for the eighteen years of her creative endeavors. When everything else soured; when a succession of therapists deserted her for whatever good, poor, or personal reasons; when intimates lost interest or could not fulfill all the roles they were asked to play; when a series of catastrophes and physical illnesses assaulted her, the making of poems remained her one constant. To use her own metaphor, "out of used furniture [she made] a tree." Without this rich, rescuing obsession I feel certain she would have succeeded in committing suicide in response to one of the dozen impulses that beset her during the period between 1957 and 1974.

Sexton's progress in Holmes's workshop in 1957 was meteoric. In short order her poems were accepted for publication in *The New Yorker, Harper's Magazine,* and the *Saturday Review.* Sam Albert was in that class, and Ruth Soter, the friend to whom "With Mercy for the Greedy" is dedicated. Through Holmes, we met George Starbuck at the New England Poetry Club. A year later, five of us joined together to form a workshop of our own — an arrangement that lasted until Holmes's untimely death from cancer in 1962. During this period, all of us wrote and revised prolifically, competitively, as if all the wolves of the world were at our backs. Our sessions were jagged, intense, often angry, but also loving. As Holmes's letters from this period make abundantly clear, he decried the confessional direction Anne's poems were taking, while at the same time acknowledging her talent. Her compulsion to deal with such then-taboo material as suicide, madness, and abortion assaulted his sensibilities and triggered his own defenses. Convinced that the relationship would harm my own work, he warned me to resist becoming involved with Anne. It was the only advice he gave me that I rejected, and at some psychic cost. Anne and I both regarded Holmes as an academic father. In desperate rebuttal, Anne wrote "For John, Who Begs Me Not to Enquire Further." A hesitant, sensitive exploration of their differences, the poem seeks to make peace between them.

Virtually every poem in the *Bedlam* book came under scrutiny during this period, as did many of the poems in *All My Pretty Ones.* There was no more determined reviser than Sexton, who would willingly push a poem through twenty or more drafts. She had an unparalleled tenacity in those early days and only abandoned a "failed" poem with regret, if not downright anger, after dozens of attempts to make it come right. It was awesome the way she could arrive at our bimonthly sessions with three, four, even five new and complicated poems. She was never meek about it, but she did listen, and she did respect the counsel of others. She gave generous help to her colleagues, and she required, demanded, insisted on generous response.

As a result of this experience, Anne came to believe in the value of the workshop. She loved growing in this way, and she urged the method on her students at Boston University, Colgate, Oberlin, and in other workshops she conducted from time to time.

During the workshop years, we began to communicate more and more frequently by telephone. Since there were no message units involved in the basic monthly phone-company fee — the figure I remember is seven dollars — we had a second phone line installed in our suburban homes so that we could talk at will. For years we conducted our own mini-workshops by phone, a working method that does much to train the ear to hear line breaks, internal rhymes, intentional or unwanted musical devices, and so forth. We did this so comfortably and over such an extended period of time that indeed when we met we were somewhat shy of each other's poems as they appeared on the page. I can remember often saying "Oh, so *that's* what it looks like," of a poem I had heard and visualized through half-a-dozen revisions.

Over the years, Anne's lines shortened, her line breaks became, I think, more unpredictable, and her imagery grew increasingly surreal. Initially, however, she worked quite strictly in traditional forms, believing in the value of their rigor as a forcing agent, believing that the hardest truths would come to light if they were made to fit a stanzaic pattern, a rhyme scheme, a prevailing meter. She strove to use rhyme unexpectedly but always aptly. Even the most unusual rhyme, she felt, must never obtrude on the sense of the line, nor must the normal word order, the easy tone of vernacular speech, be wrenched solely to save a rhyme.

The impetus for creation usually came when Anne directly invoked the muse at her desk. Here, she read favorite poems of other poets — most frequently Neruda — and played certain evocative records over and over. One I remember for its throaty string section was Respighi's "Pines of Rome." Music acted in some way to free her to create, and she often turned the volume up loud enough to drown out all other sounds.

But for all the sought-after and hard-won poems Anne wrote — in this connection, I recall the arduous struggle to complete "The Operation," "All My Pretty Ones," "Flee on Your Donkey" — a number were almost totally "given" ones. "Riding the Elevator into the Sky," in *The Awful Rowing*, is an example. The newspaper article referred to in the opening stanza suggested the poem; the poem itself came quite cleanly and easily, as if written out in the air beforehand and then transcribed onto the page with very few alterations. Similarly arrived at, "Letter Written on a Ferry While Crossing Long Island Sound" began at the instant Anne sighted the nuns on an actual crossing. The poem was written much as it now appears on the page, except for minor skirmishes required to effect the closure in each stanza. "Young" and "I Remember" were also achieved almost without effort. But because Anne wanted to open *All My Pretty Ones* with a terse elegy for her parents, one shorn of all autobiographical detail, "The Truth the Dead Know" went through innumerable revisions before arriving at its final form, an *a b a b* rhyme scheme that allows little room for pyrotechnics.

For a time, it seemed that psychiatrists all over the country were referring their patients to Anne's work, as if it could provide the balm in Gilead for every troubled person. Even though it comforted and nurtured her to know that her poems reached beyond the usual sphere of belles lettres, she felt considerable ambivalence about her subject matter. Accused of exhibitionism, she was determined only to be more flamboyant; nevertheless, the strict Puritan hiding inside her suffered and grieved over the label of "confessional poet." For instance, when she wrote "Cripples and Other Stories" (in *Live or Die*), a poem that almost totally "occurred" on the page in an hour's time, she crumpled it up and tossed it into the wastebasket as if in embarrassment. Together we fished it out and saved it, working to make the tone more consistent and to smooth out some of the rhythmically crude spots. Into this sort of mechanical task Anne always flung herself gladly.

The results were often doubly effective. I remember, for instance, how in "The Operation" she worked to achieve through rhyme and the shaping of the poem's three parts a direct rendition of the actual experience. The retardation of rhyming sounds in those short, rather sharply end-stopped lines, in the first section, for example (*leaf, straw, lawn: car, thief, house, upon*), add to the force of metaphor in the poem — the "historic thief," the "Humpty-Dumpty," and so on. Or, to take another poem, "Faustus and I," in *The Death Notebooks*, was headed for the discard pile. It was a free-verse poem at the outset and had what seemed to me a malevolently flippant tone. Often when stymied for a more articulate response to one of her poems I disliked, I suggested, "Why don't you pound it into form?" And often the experiment worked. In the case of the Faustus poem, the suggestion was useful because the rhyme scheme gave the subject a dignity it demanded and because the repetitive "pounding" elicited a level of language, of metaphor, that Anne had not quite reached in the earlier version.

Sexton had an almost mystical faith in the "found" wor as well as in metaphor by mistake, by typo, or by misap She would fight hard to keep an image, a line, a wor if I was just as dogged in my conviction that the line was sentimental or mawkish, that the word was ill image trite, she would capitulate — unless she w vinced of her own rightness. Then there was Trusting each other's critical sense, we learned n unshakable core, not to trespass on style or voice

Untrammeled by a traditional education i Yeats, Eliot, and Pound, Anne was able to s Conrad's secret sharer, for a new destiny. She lost years, her lack of a college degree; she read omnivorously and quite innocently whatever came to hand and enticed her, forming her own independent, quirky, and incisive judgments.

Searching for solutions to the depressive episodes that beset her with dismaying periodicity, Anne read widely in the popular psychiatric texts of the time: interpretations of Freud, Theodore Reik, Philip Rieff, Helena Deutsch, Erik Erikson, Bruno Bettelheim. During a summer-school course with Philip Rahv, she encountered the works of Dostoevski, Kafka, and Thomas Mann. These were succeeded by the novels of Saul Bellow, Philip Roth, and Kurt Vonnegut. But above all else, she was attracted to the fairy tales of Andersen and Grimm, which her beloved Nana had read to her when she was a child. They were for her, perhaps, what Bible stories and Greek myths had been for other writers. At the same time that she was being entertained and drawn into closer contact with a kind of collective unconscious, she was searching the fairy tales for psychological parallels. Quite unaware at first of the direction she was taking, she composed the first few "transformations" that comprise the book of that name. The book evolved very much at my urging, and gathered momentum as it grew. It struck me that Anne's poems based on fairy tales went one step further than contemporary poets' translations from languages they did not themselves read but apprehended through a third party. Their poems were *adaptations*; hers were *transformations*.

Thematically, Anne's concern in *Transformations* was a logical extension of the material she dealt with in the confessional genre, but this time with a society-mocking overlay. Her attention focuses women cast in a variety of fictive roles: the dutiful princess ghter, the wicked witch, the stepmother. We see the same constellations in a fairy-tale setting, ranging from the l explorations of "The Frog Prince" to the stage-set adultery Little Peasant." The poems are replete with anachro- m pop culture: the Queen in "Rumpelstiltskin" is "as as a Jehovah's witness"; Snow White "opened her eyes rphan Annie"; and Cinderella in her sooty rags looks like Al Jolson. Moreover, the conventional happily-ever-after endings receive their share of sardonic jibes. Cinderella and her prince end up as "Regular Bobbsey Twins./ That story." And the princess and her husband in "The White Snake" are condemned by way of a happy ending to "a kind of coffin,/ a kind of blue funk."

Despite Houghton Mifflin's initial misgivings about publishing it, *Transformations* was widely acclaimed for its balance between the confessional and the fable. It was a new lode to mine. I hoped that by encouraging Anne to continue to look outside her own psyche for material, she might develop new enthusiasms to match the one she felt for the brothers Grimm.

And indeed her impulse to work in fable continued in *The Book of Folly*, where, in addition to three prose inventions, Sexton created the sequence of poems she called "The Jesus Papers." These are more searching, more daring than the early Jesus poems ("In the Deep Museum," "For God While Sleeping," "With Mercy for the Greedy") from *All My Pretty Ones*, in which it seemed to be the cruelty of the crucifixion itself that fascinated her. Now we have a different voice and a different Jesus, however humanized, however modernized — a Jesus who still suffers knowingly in order to endure.

Jesus, Mary, angels as good as the good fairy, and a personal, fatherly God to love and forgive her, figure ever more prominently in the late poems. Always Sexton explores relentlessly the eternal themes that obsess her: love, loss, madness, the nature of the father-daughter compact, and death — the Death Baby we carry with us from the moment of birth. In my view, the sequence entitled "The Death of the Fathers," a stunning investigation of these latter two themes, is the most successful part of *The Book of Folly*. It would be simplistic to suggest that the Oedipal theme overrides all other considerations in Sexton's work, but a good case might be made for viewing her poems in terms of their quest for a male authority figure to love and trust. Yeats once said that "one poem lights up another," and in Sexton's poetry the reader can find the poet again and again identifying herself through her relationship with the male Other, whether in the person of a lover or — in the last, hasty, and often brilliant poems in *The Awful Rowing*, which make a final effort to land on "the island called God" — in the person of the patriarchal final arbiter.

The poems in *Transformations* mark the beginning of a shift in Sexton's work, from the intensely confessional to what Estella Lauter, in a fascinating essay, "Anne Sexton's 'Radical Discontent with the Order of Things,'" has termed the "transpersonal." In retrospect, it seems to me that the broad acceptance *Transformations* eventually earned in the marketplace (after hesitant beginnings) reinforced Sexton's deeply rooted conviction that poems not only could, but had to be, made out of the detritus of her life. Her work took on a new imaginative boldness. She experimented with a variety of persona/poems, particularly involving God figures, revisited the crucifixion stories, reworked the creation myth and ancient psalms, and even planned a book-length bestiary, which was only partially realized. Her perception of her place in the canon of American letters was enhanced, too, by the success of *Transformations*. Inscribing a copy of *The Book of Folly* for me in 1972, she wrote: "Dear Max — From now on it's OUR world."

She began to speak of herself as Ms. Dog, an appellation that is ironic in two contexts. We were both increasingly aware of the Women's Movement. To shuck the earlier designations of Miss and Mrs. was only a token signal of where we stood, but a signal nonetheless. Dog, of course, is God in reverse. The fact that the word worked both ways delighted Sexton much as her favorite palindrome, "rats live on no evil star," did. There was a wonderful impudence in naming herself a kind of liberated female deity, one who is "out fighting the dollars."

In the collections that followed *Transformations*, images of God proliferate, crossing all boundaries between man and woman, human and animal; between inner and outer histories of behavior. It was slippery material, difficult to control. Not all the poems Anne arrived at in this pursuit of self-definition and salvation succeed; of this she was well aware. Whenever it came down to a question of what to include, or what to drop from a forthcoming collection, Anne agonized at length. It was our practice over the years to sit quietly with each other on the occasion of the arranging of a book, sorting through groups of poems, trying out a variety of formats, voting on which poems to save and which to discard. In a kind of despondency of the moment, suffering the bitter foretaste of reviews to come, Anne frequently wanted to jettison half the book. But I suspect this was a way she had of taking the sting out of the selection process, secure in the knowledge that she and I would always rescue each other's better poems; even, for the right reasons, rescue those flawed ones that were important psychically or developmentally. We took comfort from Yeats's "lighting-up," allowing the poems to gain meaning and perspective from one another.

When Anne was writing *The Awful Rowing* at white heat in January and February of 1973, and the poems were coming at the rate of two, three, even four a day, the awesome pace terrified me. I was poet-in-residence at Centre College in Danville, Kentucky; we had agreed in advance to split the phone bill. Fearing a manic break, I did everything I could to retard the process, long-distance, during our daily hour-long calls. The Sexton who had so defiantly boasted, in her Ms. Dog phase, "I am God la de dah," had now given way to a ravaged, obsessed poet fighting to put the jigsaw pieces of the puzzle together into a coherence that would save her — into "a whole nation of God." Estella Lauter states that "her vision of Him as the winner in a crooked poker game at the end of that book is a sporting admission of her defeat rather than a decisive renewal of the Christian myth." On one level, I agree. But on another, even more primitive level, God the poker-player was the one living and constant Daddy left to Sexton out of the "Death of the Fathers." Of course he held the crooked, winning hand.

Though the reviewers were not always kind to Anne's work, honors and awards mounted piggyback on one another almost from the moment of the publication in 1960 of her first book, *To Bedlam and Part Way Back*. The American Academy of Letters Traveling Fellowship in 1963, which she was awarded shortly after *All My Pretty Ones* was published and nominated for the National Book Award, was followed by a Ford Foundation grant as resident playwright at the Charles Playhouse in Boston. In 1965, Anne Sexton was elected a Fellow of the Royal Society of Literature in Great Britain. *Live or Die* won the Pulitzer Prize in poetry in 1967. She was named Phi Beta Kappa poet at Harvard in 1968 and accorded a number of honorary doctoral degrees.

Twice in the 1960s, and twice more in the 1970s, Anne and I collaborated to write books for children. *Eggs of Things* and *More Eggs of Things* were constructed within the constraints of a limited vocabulary. *Joey and the Birthday Present* and *The Wizard's Tears* were more fanciful excursions into the realm of talking animals and magical spells. Our work sessions were lighthearted, even casual. We took turns sitting at the typewriter; whoever typed had the privilege of recording or censoring the dialogue or description as it occurred to us. Three or four afternoon workouts sufficed for a book. We were full of generous praise for each other's contributions to the story line and to the exchanges of conversation. It was usually summer. We drank a lot of iced tea and squabbled amiably about how to turn the *Wizard's* townspeople into frogs, or about which of us actually first spoke the key line in *Joey*: "And they both agreed a birthday present cannot run away." Sometimes we explored plans for future collaborations. We would do a new collection of animal fables, modeled on Aesop. We would fish out the rejected sequel to *More Eggs*, entitled *Cowboy and Pest and the Runaway Goat*, and refurbish it for another publisher. Sexton enthusiastically entertained these notions, as did I. Working together on children's books when our own children were the age of our projected readership kept us in good rapport with each other's offspring. It provided a welcome breathing space in which nothing mattered but the sheer verbal play involved in developing the story. Indeed, we regressed cheerfully to whatever age level the text required, and lost ourselves in the confabulation.

But between the publication of new books and the bestowal of honors fell all too frequently the shadow of mental illness. One psychiatrist left. His successor at first succumbed to Sexton's charm, then terminated his treatment of her. She promptly fell downstairs and broke her hip — on her birthday. With the next doctor, her hostility grew. Intermediary psychiatrists and psychologists came and went. There seemed to be no standard for dealing with this gifted, ghosted woman. On Thorazine, she gained weight, became intensely sun-sensitive, and complained that she was so overwhelmed with lassitude that she could not write. Without medication, the voices returned. As she grew increasingly dependent on alcohol, sedatives, and sleeping pills, her depressive bouts grew more frequent. Convinced that her marriage was beyond salvage, she demanded and won a divorce, only to learn that living alone created an unbearable level of anxiety. She returned to Westwood Lodge, later spent time at McLean's Hospital in Belmont, Massachusetts, and finally went to the Human Resources Institute in Brookline, Massachusetts. But none of these interludes stemmed her downward course. In the spring of 1974, she took an overdose of sleeping pills and later remonstrated bitterly with me for aborting this suicide attempt. On that occasion she vowed that when she next undertook to die, she would telegraph her intent to no one. A little more than six months later, this indeed proved to be the case.

It seems presumptuous, only seven years after her death, to talk about Anne Sexton's place in the history of poetry. We must first acknowledge the appearance in the twentieth century of women writing poetry that confronts the issues of gender, social role, and female life and lives viewed subjectively from the female perspective. The earlier world view of the poet as "the masculine chief of state in charge of dispensing universal spiritual truths" (Diane Middlebrook, *The World Into Words*) has eroded since World War II, as have earlier notions about the existence of universal truths themselves. Freed by that cataclysm from their clichéd roles as goddesses of hearth and bedroom, women began to write openly out of their own experiences. Before there was a Women's Movement, the underground river was already flowing, carrying such diverse cargoes as the poems of Bogan, Levertov, Rukeyser, Swenson, Plath, Rich, and Sexton.*

* I have omitted from this list Elizabeth Bishop, who chose not to have her work included in anthologies of women poets.

The stuff of Anne's life, mercilessly dissected, is here in the poems. Of all the confessional poets, none has had quite Sexton's "courage to make a clean breast of it." Nor has any displayed quite her brilliance, her verve, her headlong metaphoric leaps. As with any body of work, some of the later poems display only ragged, intermittent control, as compared to "The Double Image," "The Operation," and "Some Foreign Letters," to choose three arbitrary examples. The later work takes more chances, crosses more boundaries between the rational and the surreal; and time after time it evokes in the reader that sought-after shiver of recognition.

Women poets in particular owe a debt to Anne Sexton, who broke new ground, shattered taboos, and endured a barrage of attacks along the way because of the flamboyance of her subject matter, which, twenty years later, seems far less daring. She wrote openly about menstruation, abortion, masturbation, incest, adultery, and drug addiction at a time when the proprieties embraced none of these as proper topics for poetry. Today, the remonstrances seem almost quaint. Anne delineated the problematic position of women — the neurotic reality of the time — though she was not able to cope in her own life with the personal trouble it created. If it is true that she attracted the worshipful attention of a cult group pruriently interested in her suicidal impulses, her psychotic breakdowns, her frequent hospitalizations, it must equally be acknowledged that her very frankness succored many who clung to her poems as to the Holy Grail. Time will sort out the dross among these poems and burnish the gold. Anne Sexton has earned her place in the canon.

To Bedlam and Part Way Back

(1960)

To Kayo who waited

husband

It is the courage to make a clean breast of it in face of every question that makes the philosopher. He must be like Sophocles's Oedipus, who, seeking enlightenment concerning his terrible fate, pursues his indefatigable enquiry, even when he divines that appalling horror awaits him in the answer. But most of us carry in our heart the Jocasta who begs Oedipus for God's sake not to inquire further . . .

From a letter of Schopenhauer
to Goethe, November 1815

Obviously about her psychiatrist.

I

YOU, DOCTOR MARTIN

You, Doctor Martin, walk
from breakfast to madness. Late August,
I speed through the antiseptic tunnel
    where the moving dead still talk
of pushing their bones against the thrust
of cure. And I am queen of this summer hotel
    or the laughing bee on a stalk

    of death. We stand in broken
lines and wait while they unlock
the door and count us at the frozen gates
    of dinner. The shibboleth is spoken
and we move to gravy in our smock
of smiles. We chew in rows, our plates
    scratch and whine like chalk

I'm the institution describing the meals

    in school. There are no knives
for cutting your throat. I make
moccasins all morning. At first my hands
    kept empty, unraveled for the lives
they used to work. Now I learn to take
them back, each angry finger that demands
    I mend what another will break

    tomorrow. Of course, I love you;
you lean above the plastic sky,
god of our block, prince of all the foxes.
    The breaking crowns are new
that Jack wore. Your third eye

3

moves among us and lights the separate boxes
where we sleep or cry.

What large children we are
here. All over I grow most tall
in the best ward. Your business is people,
you call at the madhouse, an oracular
eye in our nest. Out in the hall
the intercom pages you. You twist in the pull
of the foxy children who fall

like floods of life in frost.
And we are magic talking to itself,
noisy and alone. I am queen of all my sins
forgotten. Am I still lost?
Once I was beautiful. Now I am myself,
counting this row and that row of moccasins
waiting on the silent shelf.

KIND SIR: THESE WOODS

For a man needs only to be turned around once
with his eyes shut in this world to be lost. . . . Not
til we are lost . . . do we begin to find ourselves.
                              THOREAU, *Walden*

Kind Sir: This is an old game
that we played when we were eight and ten.
Sometimes on The Island, in down Maine,
in late August, when the cold fog blew in
off the ocean, the forest between Dingley Dell
and grandfather's cottage grew white and strange.
It was as if every pine tree were a brown pole
we did not know; as if day had rearranged
into night and bats flew in sun. It was a trick
to turn around once and know you were lost;
knowing the crow's horn was crying in the dark,
knowing that supper would never come, that the coast's
cry of doom from that far away bell buoy's bell
said *your nursemaid is gone.* O Mademoiselle,

4

the rowboat rocked over. Then you were dead.
Turn around once, eyes tight, the thought in your head.

Kind Sir: Lost and of your same kind
I have turned around twice with my eyes sealed
and the woods were white and my night mind
saw such strange happenings, untold and unreal.
And opening my eyes, I am afraid of course
to look — this inward look that society scorns —
Still, I search in these woods and find nothing worse
than myself, caught between the grapes and the thorns.

TORN DOWN FROM GLORY DAILY

All day we watched the gulls
striking the top of the sky
and riding the blown roller coaster.
Up there
godding the whole blue world
and shrieking at a snip of land.

Now, like children,
we climb down humps of rock
with a bag of dinner rolls,
left over,
and spread them gently on a stone,
leaving six crusts for an early king.

A single watcher comes hawking in,
rides the current round its hunger
and hangs
carved in silk
until it throbs up suddenly,
out, and one inch over water;

to come again
smoothing over the slap tide.
To come bringing its flock, like a city

of wings that fall from the air.
They wait, each like a wooden decoy
or soft like a pigeon or

a sweet snug duck:
until one moves, moves that dart-beak
breaking over. It has the bread.
The world is full of them,
a world of beasts
thrusting for one rock.

Just four scoop out the bread
and go swinging over Gloucester
to the top of the sky.
Oh see how
they cushion their fishy bellies
with a brother's crumb.

MUSIC SWIMS BACK TO ME

again, about hospitalization

Wait Mister. Which way is home?
They turned the light out
and the dark is moving in the corner.
There are no sign posts in this room,
four ladies, over eighty,
in diapers every one of them.
La la la, Oh music swims back to me
and I can feel the tune they played
the night they left me
in this private institution on a hill.

Imagine it. A radio playing
and everyone here was crazy.
I liked it and danced in a circle.
Music pours over the sense
and in a funny way
music sees more than I.
I mean it remembers better;

6

remembers the first night here.
It was the strangled cold of November;
even the stars were strapped in the sky
and that moon too bright
forking through the bars to stick me
with a singing in the head.
I have forgotten all the rest.

They lock me in this chair at eight a.m.
and there are no signs to tell the way,
just the radio beating to itself
and the song that remembers
more than I. Oh, la la la,
this music swims back to me.
The night I came I danced a circle
and was not afraid.
Mister?

[handwritten annotation: she was not fearful the first night she was there b/c she didn't know about "the chair" (electric shock therapy)]

THE BELLS

Today the circus poster
is scabbing off the concrete wall
and the children have forgotten
if they knew at all.
Father, do you remember?
Only the sound remains,
the distant thump of the good elephants,
the voice of the ancient lions
and how the bells
trembled for the flying man.
I, laughing,
lifted to your high shoulder
or small at the rough legs of strangers,
was not afraid.
You held my hand
and were instant to explain
the three rings of danger.

[handwritten annotation: Remembrance of a father figure]

7

Oh see the naughty clown
and the wild parade
while love love
love grew rings around me.
This was the sound where it began;
our breath pounding up to see
the flying man breast out
across the boarded sky
and climb the air.
I remember the color of music
and how forever
all the trembling bells of you
were mine.

ELIZABETH GONE

1.

You lay in the nest of your real death,
Beyond the print of my nervous fingers
Where they touched your moving head;
Your old skin puckering, your lungs' breath
Grown baby short as you looked up last
At my face swinging over the human bed,
And somewhere you cried, *let me go let me go.*

You lay in the crate of your last death,
But were not you, not finally you.
They have stuffed her cheeks, I said;
This clay hand, this mask of Elizabeth
Are not true. From within the satin
And the suede of this inhuman bed,
Something cried, *let me go let me go.*

2.

They gave me your ash and bony shells,
Rattling like gourds in the cardboard urn,

Rattling like stones that their oven had blest.
I waited you in the cathedral of spells
And I waited you in the country of the living,
Still with the urn crooned to my breast,
When something cried, *let me go let me go.*

So I threw out your last bony shells
And heard me scream for the look of you,
Your apple face, the simple crèche
Of your arms, the August smells
Of your skin. Then I sorted your clothes
And the loves you had left, Elizabeth,
Elizabeth, until you were gone.

SOME FOREIGN LETTERS

I knew you forever and you were always old,
soft white lady of my heart. Surely you would scold
me for sitting up late, reading your letters,
as if these foreign postmarks were meant for me.
You posted them first in London, wearing furs
and a new dress in the winter of eighteen-ninety.
I read how London is dull on Lord Mayor's Day,
where you guided past groups of robbers, the sad holes
of Whitechapel, clutching your pocketbook, on the way
to Jack the Ripper dissecting his famous bones.
This Wednesday in Berlin, you say, you will
go to a bazaar at Bismarck's house. And I
see you as a young girl in a good world still,
writing three generations before mine. I try
to reach into your page and breathe it back . . .
but life is a trick, life is a kitten in a sack.

This is the sack of time your death vacates.
How distant you are on your nickel-plated skates
in the skating park in Berlin, gliding past
me with your Count, while a military band
plays a Strauss waltz. I loved you last,

a pleated old lady with a crooked hand.
Once you read Lohengrin and every goose
hung high while you practiced castle life
in Hanover. Tonight your letters reduce
history to a guess. The Count had a wife.
You were the old maid aunt who lived with us.
Tonight I read how the winter howled around
the towers of Schloss Schwöbber, how the tedious
language grew in your jaw, how you loved the sound
of the music of the rats tapping on the stone
floors. When you were mine you wore an earphone.

This is Wednesday, May 9th, near Lucerne,
Switzerland, sixty-nine years ago. I learn
your first climb up Mount San Salvatore;
this is the rocky path, the hole in your shoes,
the yankee girl, the iron interior
of her sweet body. You let the Count choose
your next climb. You went together, armed
with alpine stocks, with ham sandwiches
and seltzer wasser. You were not alarmed
by the thick woods of briars and bushes,
nor the rugged cliff, nor the first vertigo
up over Lake Lucerne. The Count sweated
with his coat off as you waded through top snow.
He held your hand and kissed you. You rattled
down on the train to catch a steamboat for home;
or other postmarks: Paris, Verona, Rome.

This is Italy. You learn its mother tongue.
I read how you walked on the Palatine among
the ruins of the palaces of the Caesars;
alone in the Roman autumn, alone since July.
When you were mine they wrapped you out of here
with your best hat over your face. I cried
because I was seventeen. I am older now.
I read how your student ticket admitted you
into the private chapel of the Vatican and how

10

you cheered with the others, as we used to do
on the Fourth of July. One Wednesday in November
you watched a balloon, painted like a silver ball,
float up over the Forum, up over the lost emperors,
to shiver its little modern cage in an occasional
breeze. You worked your New England conscience out
beside artisans, chestnut vendors and the devout.

Tonight I will learn to love you twice;
learn your first days, your mid-Victorian face.
Tonight I will speak up and interrupt
your letters, warning you that wars are coming,
that the Count will die, that you will accept
your America back to live like a prim thing
on the farm in Maine. I tell you, you will come
here, to the suburbs of Boston, to see the blue-nose
world go drunk each night, to see the handsome
children jitterbug, to feel your left ear close
one Friday at Symphony. And I tell you,
you will tip your boot feet out of that hall,
rocking from its sour sound, out onto
the crowded street, letting your spectacles fall
and your hair net tangle as you stop passers-by
to mumble your guilty love while your ears die.

THE KITE
West Harwich, Massachusetts, 1954–1959

Here, in front of the summer hotel
the beach waits like an altar.
We are lying on a cloth of sand
while the Atlantic noon stains
the world in light.

           It was much the same
five years ago. I remember
how Ezio Pinza was flying a kite

11

for the children. None of us noticed
it then. The pleated lady
was still a nest of her knitting.
Four pouchy fellows kept their policy
of gin and tonic while trading some money.
The parasol girls slept, sun-sitting
their lovely years. No one thought
how precious it was, or even how funny
the festival seemed, square rigged in the air.
The air was a season they had bought,
like the cloth of sand.

                    I've been waiting
on this private stretch of summer land,
counting these five years and wondering why.
I mean, it was different that time
with Ezio Pinza flying a kite.
Maybe, after all, he knew something more
and was right.

SAID THE POET TO THE ANALYST

My business is words. Words are like labels,
or coins, or better, like swarming bees.
I confess I am only broken by the sources of things;
as if words were counted like dead bees in the attic,
unbuckled from their yellow eyes and their dry wings.
I must always forget how one word is able to pick
out another, to manner another, until I have got
something I might have said . . .
but did not.

Your business is watching my words. But I
admit nothing. I work with my best, for instance,
when I can write my praise for a nickel machine,
that one night in Nevada: telling how the magic jackpot
came clacking three bells out, over the lucky screen.

12

But if you should say this is something it is not,
then I grow weak, remembering how my hands felt funny
and ridiculous and crowded with all
the believing money.

VENUS AND THE ARK

The missile to launch a missile
was almost a secret.
Two male Ph.D.'s were picked
and primed to fill it
and one hundred
carefully counted insects,
three almost new snakes,
coiled in a cube,
exactly fifty fish creatures
in tanks, the necessary files,
twenty bars of food, ten brief cures,
special locks, fourteen white rats,
fourteen black rats, a pouch of dirt,
were all stuffed aboard before
the thing blasted from the desert.

parallel to man walking on the moon

And the missile that launched
a missile launched out
into a marvelous scientific balloon
that rolled and bobbed about
in the mists of Venus; suddenly
sank like a sweet fat grape,
oozing past gravity to snuggle
down upon the triumphant shape
of space. The two men signaled
Earth, telling their Continent
VENUS IS GREEN. And parades assembled,
the loud earth tellers spent
all fifteen minutes on it, even
shortened their weather forecast.

But rival nations, angry and oily,
fired up their best atom blast
and the last Earth war was done.
The place became crater on each side,
sank down to its first skull,
shedding forests, oceans, dried
bones and neons, as it fell through
time like a forgotten pitted stone.

These two men walked hopefully out
onto their hot empty planet
with machines, rats, tanks,
boxes, insects and the one odd set
of three almost new snakes,
to make the tests they were meant to do.
But on the seventh month the cages
grew small, too small to interview,
too tight to bear. The rats were gray
and heavy things where they ran
against wire and the snakes built eggs
on eggs and even the fish began
to bump in water as they spawned
on every side of each other's swim.
And the men grew listless; they opened
the pouch of dirt, undid each locked bin
and let every creature loose
to live on Venus, or anyhow hide
under rocks. Bees swarmed the air,
letting a warm pollen slide
from their wings and onto the grass.
The fish flapped to a small pool
and the rats untangled their hairs
and humped over the vestibule
of the cramped balloon. Trees sprang
from lichen, the rock became a park,
where, even at star-time, things brushed;
even in the planet's new dark
crotch, that air snag where snakes
coupled and rats rubbed in disrepair,

Russian American race

14

it grew quick and noisy with
a kind of wonder in the lonely air.

Old and withered, two Ph.D.'s
from Earth hobbled slowly back
to their empty balloon, crying alone
for sense, for the troubling lack
of something they ought to do,
while countless fish slapped
and the waters grew, green came
taller and the happy rats sped
through integrated forests,
barking like dogs at the top
of the sky. But the two men,
that last morning of death, before
the first of light, watched the land
of Venus, its sweetless shore,
and thought, "This is the end.
This is the last of a man like me."
Until they saw, over the mists
of Venus, two fish creatures stop
on spangled legs and crawl
from the belly of the sea.
And from the planet park
they heard the new fruit drop.

HER KIND — *possibly comparing herself to the women in the Salem Witch Trials*

I have gone out, a possessed witch,
haunting the black air, braver at night;
dreaming evil, I have done my hitch
over the plain houses, light by light:
lonely thing, twelve-fingered, out of mind.
A woman like that is not a woman, quite.
I have been her kind.

I have found the warm caves in the woods,
filled them with skillets, carvings, shelves,
closets, silks, innumerable goods;
fixed the suppers for the worms and the elves:
whining, rearranging the disaligned.
A woman like that is misunderstood.
I have been her kind.

I have ridden in your cart, driver,
waved my nude arms at villages going by,
learning the last bright routes, survivor
where your flames still bite my thigh
and my ribs crack where your wheels wind.
A woman like that is not ashamed to die.
I have been her kind.

reference to being burned at the stake?

THE EXORCISTS

And I solemnly swear
on the chill of secrecy
that I know you not, this room never,
the swollen dress I wear,
nor the anonymous spoons that free me,
nor this calendar nor the pulse we pare and cover.

For all these present,
before that wandering ghost,
that yellow moth of my summer bed,
I say: this small event
is not. So I prepare, am dosed
in ether and will not cry what stays unsaid.

I was brown with August,
the clapping waves at my thighs
and a storm riding into the cove. We swam
while the others beached and burst
for their boarded huts, their hale cries
shouting back to us and the hollow slam

of the dory against the float.
Black arms of thunder strapped
upon us; squalled out, we breathed in rain
and stroked past the boat.
We thrashed for shore as if we were trapped
in green and that suddenly inadequate stain

of lightning belling around
our skin. Bodies in air
we raced for the empty lobsterman-shack.
It was yellow inside, the sound
of the underwing of the sun. I swear,
I most solemnly swear, on all the bric-à-brac

of summer loves, I know
you not.

WHERE I LIVE IN THIS HONORABLE
HOUSE OF THE LAUREL TREE

I live in my wooden legs and O
my green green hands.
Too late
to wish I had not run from you, Apollo,
blood moves still in my bark bound veins.
I, who ran nymph foot to root in flight,
have only this late desire to arm the trees
I lie within. The measure that I have lost
silks my pulse. Each century the trickeries
of need pain me everywhere.
Frost taps my skin and I stay glossed
in honor for you are gone in time. The air
rings for you, for that astonishing rite
of my breathing tent undone within your light.
I only know how this untimely lust has tossed
flesh at the wind forever and moved my fears
toward the intimate Rome of the myth we crossed.
I am a fist of my unease

as I spill toward the stars in the empty years.
I build the air with the crown of honor; it keys
my out of time and luckless appetite.
You gave me honor too soon, Apollo.
There is no one left who understands
how I wait
here in my wooden legs and O
my green green hands.

PORTRAIT OF AN OLD WOMAN ON THE COLLEGE TAVERN WALL

Oh down at the tavern
the children are singing
around their round table
and around me still.
Did you hear what it said?

I only said
how there is a pewter urn
pinned to the tavern wall,
as old as old is able
to be and be there still.
I said, the poets are there
I hear them singing and lying
around their round table
and around me still.
Across the room is a wreath
made of a corpse's hair,
framed in glass on the wall,
as old as old is able
to be and be remembered still.
Did you hear what it said?

I only said
how I want to be there and I
would sing my songs with the liars
and my lies with all the singers.

18

And I would, and I would but
it's my hair in the hair wreath,
my cup pinned to the tavern wall,
my dusty face they sing beneath.
Poets are sitting in my kitchen.
Why do these poets lie?
Why do children get children and
Did you hear what it said?

       I only said
how I want to be there,
Oh, down at the tavern
where the prophets are singing
around their round table
until they are still.

THE FARMER'S WIFE

From the hodge porridge
of their country lust,
their local life in Illinois,
where all their acres look
like a sprouting broom factory,
they name just ten years now
that she has been his habit;
as again tonight he'll say
honey bunch let's go
and she will not say how there
must be more to living
than this brief bright bridge
of the raucous bed or even
the slow braille touch of him
like a heavy god grown light,
that old pantomime of love
that she wants although
it leaves her still alone,
built back again at last,
mind's apart from him, living

her own self in her own words
and hating the sweat of the house
they keep when they finally lie
each in separate dreams
and then how she watches him,
still strong in the blowzy bag
of his usual sleep while
her young years bungle past
their same marriage bed
and she wishes him cripple, or poet,
or even lonely, or sometimes,
better, my lover, dead.

FUNNEL

The family story tells, and it was told true,
of my great-grandfather who begat eight
genius children and bought twelve almost new
grand pianos. He left a considerable estate
when he died. The children honored their
separate arts; two became moderately famous,
three married and fattened their delicate share
of wealth and brilliance. The sixth one was
a concert pianist. She had a notable career
and wore cropped hair and walked like a man,
or so I heard when prying a childhood car
into the hushed talk of the straight Maine clan.
One died a pinafore child, she stays her five
years forever. And here is one that wrote —
I sort his odd books and wonder his once alive
words and scratch out my short marginal notes
and finger my accounts.

Back from that great-grandfather I have come
to tidy a country graveyard for his sake,
to chat with the custodian under a yearly sun
and touch a ghost sound where it lies awake.

I like best to think of that Bunyan man
slapping his thighs and trading the yankee sale
for one dozen grand pianos. It fit his plan
of culture to do it big. On this same scale
he built seven arking houses and they still stand.
One, five stories up, straight up like a square
box, still dominates its costal edge of land.
It is rented cheap in the summer musted air
to sneaker-footed families who pad through
its rooms and sometimes finger the yellow keys
of an old piano that wheezes bells of mildew.
Like a shoe factory amid the spruce trees
it squats; flat roof and rows of windows spying
through the mist. Where those eight children danced
their starfished summers, the thirty-six pines sighing,
that bearded man walked giant steps and chanced
his gifts in numbers.

Back from that great-grandfather I have come
to puzzle a bending gravestone for his sake,
to question this diminishing and feed a minimum
of children their careful slice of suburban cake.

THE EXPATRIATES

My dear, it was a moment
to clutch at for a moment
so that you may believe in it
and believing is the act of love, I think,
even in the telling, wherever it went.

In the false New England forest
where the misplanted Norwegian trees
refused to root, their thick synthetic
roots barging out of the dirt to work the air,
we held hands and walked on our knees.
Actually, there was no one there.

For forty years this experimental
woodland grew, shaft by shaft in perfect rows
where its stub branches held and its spokes fell.
It was a place of parallel trees, their lives
filed out in exile where we walked too alien to know
our sameness and how our sameness survives.

Outside of us the village cars followed
the white line we had carefully walked
two nights before toward our single beds.
We lay halfway up an ugly hill and if we fell
it was here in the woods where the woods were caught
in their dying and you held me well.

And now I must dream the forest whole
and your sweet hands, not once as frozen
as those stopped trees, nor ruled, nor pale,
nor leaving mine. Today, in my house, I see
our house, its pillars a dim basement of men
holding up their foreign ground for you and me.

My dear, it was a time,
butchered from time,
that we must tell of quickly
before we lose the sound of our own
mouths calling mine, mine, mine.

FOR JOHNNY POLE
ON THE FORGOTTEN BEACH

In his tenth July some instinct
taught him to arm the waiting wave,
a giant where its mouth hung open.
He rode on the lip that buoyed him there
and buckled him under. The beach was strung
with children paddling their ages in,
under the glare of noon chipping

22

its light out. He stood up, anonymous
and straight among them, between
their sand pails and nursery crafts.
The breakers cartwheeled in and over
to puddle their toes and test their perfect
skin. He was my brother, my small
Johnny brother, almost ten. We flopped
down upon a towel to grind the sand
under us and watched the Atlantic sea
move fire, like night sparklers;
and lost our weight in the festival
season. He dreamed, he said, to be
a man designed like a balanced wave . . .
how someday he would wait, giant
and straight.

Johnny, your dream moves summers
inside my mind.

He was tall and twenty that July,
but there was no balance to help;
only the shells came straight and even.
This was the first beach of assault;
the odor of death hung in the air
like rotting potatoes; the junkyard
of landing craft waited open and rusting.
The bodies were strung out as if they were
still reaching for each other, where they lay
to blacken, to burst through their perfect
skin. And Johnny Pole was one of them.
He gave in like a small wave, a sudden
hole in his belly and the years all gone
where the Pacific noon chipped its light out.
Like a bean bag, outflung, head loose
and anonymous, he lay. Did the sea move fire
for its battle season? Does he lie there
forever, where his rifle waits, giant
and straight? . . . I think you die again
and live again,

Johnny, each summer that moves inside
my mind.

UNKNOWN GIRL IN
THE MATERNITY WARD

Child, the current of your breath is six days long.
You lie, a small knuckle on my white bed;
lie, fisted like a snail, so small and strong
at my breast. Your lips are animals; you are fed
with love. At first hunger is not wrong.
The nurses nod their caps; you are shepherded
down starch halls with the other unnested throng
in wheeling baskets. You tip like a cup; your head
moving to my touch. You sense the way we belong.
But this is an institution bed.
You will not know me very long.

The doctors are enamel. They want to know
the facts. They guess about the man who left me,
some pendulum soul, going the way men go
and leave you full of child. But our case history
stays blank. All I did was let you grow.
Now we are here for all the ward to see.
They thought I was strange, although
I never spoke a word. I burst empty
of you, letting you learn how the air is so.
The doctors chart the riddle they ask of me
and I turn my head away. I do not know.

Yours is the only face I recognize.
Bone at my bone, you drink my answers in.
Six times a day I prize
your need, the animals of your lips, your skin
growing warm and plump. I see your eyes
lifting their tents. They are blue stones, they begin
to outgrow their moss. You blink in surprise

and I wonder what you can see, my funny kin,
as you trouble my silence. I am a shelter of lies.
Should I learn to speak again, or hopeless in
such sanity will I touch some face I recognize?

Down the hall the baskets start back. My arms
fit you like a sleeve, they hold
catkins of your willows, the wild bee farms
of your nerves, each muscle and fold
of your first days. Your old man's face disarms
the nurses. But the doctors return to scold
me. I speak. It is you my silence harms.
I should have known; I should have told
them something to write down. My voice alarms
my throat. "Name of father—none." I hold
you and name you bastard in my arms.

And now that's that. There is nothing more
that I can say or lose.
Others have traded life before
and could not speak. I tighten to refuse
your owling eyes, my fragile visitor.
I touch your cheeks, like flowers. You bruise
against me. We unlearn. I am a shore
rocking you off. You break from me. I choose
your only way, my small inheritor
and hand you off, trembling the selves we lose.
Go child, who is my sin and nothing more.

WHAT'S THAT

Before it came inside
I had watched it from my kitchen window,
watched it swell like a new balloon,
watched it slump and then divide,
like something I know I know —
a broken pear or two halves of the moon,

or round white plates floating nowhere
or fat hands waving in the summer air
until they fold together like a fist or a knee.
After that it came to my door. Now it lives here.
And of course: it is a soft sound, soft as a seal's ear,
that was caught between a shape and a shape and then returned to me.

You know how parents call
from sweet beaches anywhere, *come in come in,*
and how you sank under water to put out
the sound, or how one of them touched in the hall
at night: the rustle and the skin
you couldn't know, but heard, the stout
slap of tides and the dog snoring. It's here
now, caught back from time in my adult year —
the image we did forget: the cranking shells on our feet
or the swing of the spoon in soup. It is as real
as splinters stuck in your ear. The noise we steal
is half a bell. And outside cars whisk by on the suburban street

and are there and are true.
What else is this, this intricate shape of air?
calling me, calling you.

THE MOSS OF HIS SKIN

Young girls in old Arabia were often buried alive next
to their dead fathers, apparently as sacrifice to the
goddesses of the tribes . . .
        HAROLD FELDMAN, "Children of the Desert"
        Psychoanalysis and Psychoanalytic Review, Fall 1958

It was only important
to smile and hold still,
to lie down beside him
and to rest awhile,
to be folded up together
as if we were silk,
to sink from the eyes of mother
and not to talk.
The black room took us

like a cave or a mouth
or an indoor belly.
I held my breath
and daddy was there,
his thumbs, his fat skull,
his teeth, his hair growing
like a field or a shawl.
I lay by the moss
of his skin until
it grew strange. My sisters
will never know that I fall
out of myself and pretend
that Allah will not see
how I hold my daddy
like an old stone tree.

HUTCH

of her arms, this was her sin:
where the wood berries bin
of forest was new and full,
she crept out by its tall
posts, those wooden legs,
and heard the sound of wild pigs

calling and did not wait nor care.
The leaves wept in her hair
as she sank to a pit of needles
and twisted out the ivyless
gate, where the wood berries bin
was full and a pig came in.

NOON WALK ON THE ASYLUM LAWN

The summer sun ray
shifts through a suspicious tree.
though I walk through the valley of the shadow

It sucks the air
and looks around for me.

The grass speaks.
I hear green chanting all day.
I will fear no evil, fear no evil
The blades extend
and reach my way.

The sky breaks.
It sags and breathes upon my face.
in the presence of mine enemies, mine enemies
The world is full of enemies.
There is no safe place.

RINGING THE BELLS

And this is the way they ring
the bells in Bedlam
and this is the bell-lady
who comes each Tuesday morning
to give us a music lesson
and because the attendants make you go
and because we mind by instinct,
like bees caught in the wrong hive,
we are the circle of the crazy ladies
who sit in the lounge of the mental house
and smile at the smiling woman
who passes us each a bell,
who points at my hand
that holds my bell, E flat,
and this is the gray dress next to me
who grumbles as if it were special
to be old, to be old,
and this is the small hunched squirrel girl
on the other side of me
who picks at the hairs over her lip,
who picks at the hairs over her lip all day,

and this is how the bells really sound,
as untroubled and clean
as a workable kitchen,
and this is always my bell responding
to my hand that responds to the lady
who points at me, E flat;
and although we are no better for it,
they tell you to go. And you do.

LULLABY

It is a summer evening.
The yellow moths sag
against the locked screens
and the faded curtains
suck over the window sills
and from another building
a goat calls in his dreams.
This is the TV parlor
in the best ward at Bedlam.
The night nurse is passing
out the evening pills.
She walks on two erasers,
padding by us one by one.

My sleeping pill is white.
It is a splendid pearl;
it floats me out of myself,
my stung skin as alien
as a loose bolt of cloth.
I will ignore the bed.
I am linen on a shelf.
Let the others moan in secret;
let each lost butterfly
go home. Old woolen head,
take me like a yellow moth
while the goat calls hush-
a-bye.

THE LOST INGREDIENT

Almost yesterday, those gentle ladies stole
to their baths in Atlantic City, for the lost
rites of the first sea of the first salt
running from a faucet. I have heard they sat
for hours in briny tubs, patting hotel towels
sweetly over shivered skin, smelling the stale
harbor of a lost ocean, praying at last
for impossible loves, or new skin, or still
another child. And since this was the style,
I don't suppose they knew what they had lost.

Almost yesterday, pushing West, I lost
ten Utah driving minutes, stopped to steal
past postcard vendors, crossed the hot slit
of macadam to touch the marvelous loosed
bobbing of The Salt Lake, to honor and assault
it in its proof, to wash away some slight
need for Maine's coast. Later the funny salt
itched in my pores and stung like bees or sleet.
I rinsed it off in Reno and hurried to steal
a better proof at tables where I always lost.

Today is made of yesterday, each time I steal
toward rites I do not know, waiting for the lost
ingredient, as if salt or money or even lust
would keep us calm and prove us whole at last.

THE ROAD BACK

The car is heavy with children
tugged back from summer,
swept out of their laughing beach,
swept out while a persistent rumor
tells them nothing ends.
Today we fret and pull

on wheels, ignore our regular loss
of time, count cows and others
while the sun moves over
like an old albatross
we must not count nor kill.

There is no word for time.
Today we will
not think to number another summer
or watch its white bird into the ground.
Today, all cars,
all fathers, all mothers, all
children and lovers will
have to forget
about that thing in the sky,
going around
like a persistent rumor
that will get us yet.

THE WAITING HEAD

If I am really walking with ordinary habit
past the same rest home on the same local street
and see another waiting head at that upper front window,
just as she would always sit,
watching for anyone from her wooden seat,
then anything can be true. I only know

how each night she wrote in her leather books
that no one came. Surely I remember the hooks

of her fingers curled on mine, though even now
will not admit the times I did avoid this street,
where she lived on and on like a bleached fig
and forgot us anyhow;
visiting the pulp of her kiss, bending to repeat
each favor, trying to comb out her mossy wig

and forcing love to last. Now she is always dead
and the leather books are mine. Today I see the head

move, like some pitted angel, in that high window.
What is the waiting head doing? It looks the same.
Will it lean forward as I turn to go?
I think I hear it call to me below
but *no one came no one came.*

ELEGY IN THE CLASSROOM

In the thin classroom, where your face
was noble and your words were all things,
I find this boily creature in your place;

find you disarranged, squatting on the window sill,
irrefutably placed up there,
like a hunk of some big frog
watching us through the V
of your woolen legs.

Even so, I must admire your skill.
You are so gracefully insane.
We fidget in our plain chairs
and pretend to catalogue
our facts for your burly sorcery

or ignore your fat blind eyes
or the prince you ate yesterday
who was wise, wise, wise.

A STORY FOR ROSE ON THE
MIDNIGHT FLIGHT TO BOSTON

Until tonight they were separate specialties,
different stories, the best of their own worst.
Riding my warm cabin home, I remember Betsy's
laughter; she laughed as you did, Rose, at the first
story. Someday, I promised her, I'll be someone
going somewhere and we plotted it in the humdrum
school for proper girls. The next April the plane
bucked me like a horse, my elevators turned
and fear blew down my throat, that last profane
gauge of a stomach coming up. And then returned
to land, as unlovely as any seasick sailor,
sincerely eighteen; my first story, my funny failure.
Maybe Rose, there is always another story,
better unsaid, grim or flat or predatory.

Half a mile down the lights of the in-between cities
turn up their eyes at me. And I remember Betsy's
story; the April night of the civilian air crash
and her sudden name misspelled in the evening paper,
the interior of shock and the paper gone in the trash
ten years now. She used the return ticket I gave her.
This was the rude kill of her; two planes cracking
in mid-air over Washington, like blind birds.
And the picking up afterwards, the morticians tracking
bodies in the Potomac and piecing them like boards
to make a leg or a face. There is only her miniature
photograph left, too long ago now for fear to remember.
Special tonight because I made her into a story
that I grew to know and savor.

                         A reason to worry,
Rose, when you fix on an old death like that,
and outliving the impact, to find you've pretended.
We bank over Boston. I am safe. I put on my hat.
I am almost someone going home. The story has ended.

II

FOR JOHN, WHO BEGS ME NOT TO ENQUIRE FURTHER

Not that it was beautiful,
but that, in the end, there was
a certain sense of order there;
something worth learning
in that narrow diary of my mind,
in the commonplaces of the asylum
where the cracked mirror
or my own selfish death
outstared me.
And if I tried
to give you something else,
something outside of myself,
you would not know
that the worst of anyone
can be, finally,
an accident of hope.
I tapped my own head;
it was glass, an inverted bowl.
It is a small thing
to rage in your own bowl.
At first it was private.
Then it was more than myself;
it was you, or your house
or your kitchen.
And if you turn away
because there is no lesson here
I will hold my awkward bowl,
with all its cracked stars shining

like a complicated lie,
and fasten a new skin around it
as if I were dressing an orange
or a strange sun.
Not that it was beautiful,
but that I found some order there.
There ought to be something special
for someone
in this kind of hope.
This is something I would never find
in a lovelier place, my dear,
although your fear is anyone's fear,
like an invisible veil between us all . . .
and sometimes in private,
my kitchen, your kitchen,
my face, your face.

THE DOUBLE IMAGE

1.

I am thirty this November.
You are still small, in your fourth year.
We stand watching the yellow leaves go queer,
flapping in the winter rain,
falling flat and washed. And I remember
mostly the three autumns you did not live here.
They said I'd never get you back again.
I tell you what you'll never really know:
all the medical hypothesis
that explained my brain will never be as true as these
struck leaves letting go.

I, who chose two times
to kill myself, had said your nickname
the mewling months when you first came;
until a fever rattled
in your throat and I moved like a pantomime

above your head. Ugly angels spoke to me. The blame,
I heard them say, was mine. They tattled
like green witches in my head, letting doom
leak like a broken faucet;
as if doom had flooded my belly and filled your bassinet,
an old debt I must assume.

Death was simpler than I'd thought.
The day life made you well and whole
I let the witches take away my guilty soul.
I pretended I was dead
until the white men pumped the poison out,
putting me armless and washed through the rigamarole
of talking boxes and the electric bed.
I laughed to see the private iron in that hotel.
Today the yellow leaves
go queer. You ask me where they go. I say today believed
in itself, or else it fell.

Today, my small child, Joyce,
love your self's self where it lives.
There is no special God to refer to; or if there is,
why did I let you grow
in another place. You did not know my voice
when I came back to call. All the superlatives
of tomorrow's white tree and mistletoe
will not help you know the holidays you had to miss.
The time I did not love
myself, I visited your shoveled walks; you held my glove.
There was new snow after this.

2.

They sent me letters with news
of you and I made moccasins that I would never use.
When I grew well enough to tolerate
myself, I lived with my mother. Too late,
too late, to live with your mother, the witches said.

36

But I didn't leave. I had my portrait
done instead.

Part way back from Bedlam
I came to my mother's house in Gloucester,
Massachusetts. And this is how I came
to catch at her; and this is how I lost her.
I cannot forgive your suicide, my mother said.
And she never could. She had my portrait
done instead.

I lived like an angry guest,
like a partly mended thing, an outgrown child.
I remember my mother did her best.
She took me to Boston and had my hair restyled.
Your smile is like your mother's, the artist said.
I didn't seem to care. I had my portrait
done instead.

There was a church where I grew up
with its white cupboards where they locked us up,
row by row, like puritans or shipmates
singing together. My father passed the plate.
Too late to be forgiven now, the witches said.
I wasn't exactly forgiven. They had my portrait
done instead.

3.

All that summer sprinklers arched
over the seaside grass.
We talked of drought
while the salt-parched
field grew sweet again. To help time pass
I tried to mow the lawn
and in the morning I had my portrait done,
holding my smile in place, till it grew formal.

Once I mailed you a picture of a rabbit
and a postcard of Motif number one,
as if it were normal
to be a mother and be gone.

They hung my portrait in the chill
north light, matching
me to keep me well.
Only my mother grew ill.
She turned from me, as if death were catching,
as if death transferred,
as if my dying had eaten inside of her.
That August you were two, but I timed my days with doubt.
On the first of September she looked at me
and said I gave her cancer.
They carved her sweet hills out
and still I couldn't answer.

4.

That winter she came
part way back
from her sterile suite
of doctors, the seasick
cruise of the X-ray,
the cells' arithmetic
gone wild. Surgery incomplete,
the fat arm, the prognosis poor, I heard
them say.

During the sea blizzards
she had her
own portrait painted.
A cave of a mirror
placed on the south wall;
matching smile, matching contour.
And you resembled me; unacquainted

with my face, you wore it. But you were mine
after all.

I wintered in Boston,
childless bride,
nothing sweet to spare
with witches at my side.
I missed your babyhood,
tried a second suicide,
tried the sealed hotel a second year.
On April Fool you fooled me. We laughed and this
was good.

5.

I checked out for the last time
on the first of May;
graduate of the mental cases,
with my analyst's okay,
my complete book of rhymes,
my typewriter and my suitcases.

All that summer I learned life
back into my own
seven rooms, visited the swan boats,
the market, answered the phone,
served cocktails as a wife
should, made love among my petticoats

and August tan. And you came each
weekend. But I lie.
You seldom came. I just pretended
you, small piglet, butterfly
girl with jelly bean cheeks,
disobedient three, my splendid

stranger. And I had to learn
why I would rather

die than love, how your innocence
would hurt and how I gather
guilt like a young intern
his symptoms, his certain evidence.

That October day we went
to Gloucester the red hills
reminded me of the dry red fur fox
coat I played in as a child; stock-still
like a bear or a tent,
like a great cave laughing or a red fur fox.

We drove past the hatchery,
the hut that sells bait,
past Pigeon Cove, past the Yacht Club, past Squall's
Hill, to the house that waits
still, on the top of the sea,
and two portraits hang on opposite walls.

6.

In north light, my smile is held in place,
the shadow marks my bone.
What could I have been dreaming as I sat there,
all of me waiting in the eyes, the zone
of the smile, the young face,
the foxes' snare.

In south light, her smile is held in place,
her cheeks wilting like a dry
orchid; my mocking mirror, my overthrown
love, my first image. She eyes me from that face,
that stony head of death
I had outgrown.

The artist caught us at the turning;
we smiled in our canvas home
before we chose our foreknown separate ways.
The dry red fur fox coat was made for burning.

I rot on the wall, my own
Dorian Gray.

And this was the cave of the mirror,
that double woman who stares
at herself, as if she were petrified
in time — two ladies sitting in umber chairs.
You kissed your grandmother
and she cried.

7.

I could not get you back
except for weekends. You came
each time, clutching the picture of a rabbit
that I had sent you. For the last time I unpack
your things. We touch from habit.
The first visit you asked my name.
Now you stay for good. I will forget
how we bumped away from each other like marionettes
on strings. It wasn't the same
as love, letting weekends contain
us. You scrape your knee. You learn my name,
wobbling up the sidewalk, calling and crying.
You call me *mother* and I remember my mother again,
somewhere in greater Boston, dying.

I remember we named you Joyce
so we could call you Joy.
You came like an awkward guest
that first time, all wrapped and moist
and strange at my heavy breast.
I needed you. I didn't want a boy,
only a girl, a small milky mouse
of a girl, already loved, already loud in the house
of herself. We named you Joy.
I, who was never quite sure
about being a girl, needed another

life, another image to remind me.
And this was my worst guilt; you could not cure
nor soothe it. I made you to find me.

THE DIVISION OF PARTS

1.

Mother, my Mary Gray,
once resident of Gloucester
and Essex County,
a photostat of your will
arrived in the mail today.
This is the division of money.
I am one third
of your daughters counting my bounty
or I am a queen alone
in the parlor still,
eating the bread and honey.
It is Good Friday.
Black birds pick at my window sill.

Your coat in my closet,
your bright stones on my hand,
the gaudy fur animals
I do not know how to use,
settle on me like a debt.
A week ago, while the hard March gales
beat on your house,
we sorted your things: obstacles
of letters, family silver,
eyeglasses and shoes.
Like some unseasoned Christmas, its scales
rigged and reset,
I bundled out with gifts I did not choose.

Now the hours of The Cross
rewind. In Boston, the devout

work their cold knees
toward that sweet martyrdom
that Christ planned. My timely loss
is too customary to note; and yet
I planned to suffer
and I cannot. It does not please
my yankee bones to watch
where the dying is done
in its ugly hours. Black birds peck
at my window glass
and Easter will take its ragged son.

The clutter of worship
that you taught me, Mary Gray,
is old. I imitate
a memory of belief
that I do not own. I trip
on your death and Jesus, my stranger
floats up over
my Christian home, wearing his straight
thorn tree. I have cast my lot
and am one third thief
of you. Time, that rearranger
of estates, equips
me with your garments, but not with grief.

2.

This winter when
cancer began its ugliness
I grieved with you each day
for three months
and found you in your private nook
of the medicinal palace
for New England Women
and never once
forgot how long it took.

I read to you
from *The New Yorker*, ate suppers
you wouldn't eat, fussed
with your flowers,
joked with your nurses, as if I
were the balm among lepers,
as if I could undo
a life in hours
if I never said goodbye.

But you turned old,
all your fifty-eight years sliding
like masks from your skull;
and at the end
I packed your nightgowns in suitcases,
paid the nurses, came riding
home as if I'd been told
I could pretend
people live in places.

3.

Since then I have pretended ease,
loved with the trickeries of need, but not enough
to shed my daughterhood
or sweeten him as a man.
I drink the five o'clock martinis
and poke at this dry page like a rough
goat. Fool! I fumble my lost childhood
for a mother and lounge in sad stuff
with love to catch and catch as catch can.

And Christ still waits. I have tried
to exorcise the memory of each event
and remain still, a mixed child,
heavy with cloths of you.
Sweet witch, you are my worried guide.